RICHARD ATTENBOROUGH'S CRY FREEDOM

THE BODLEY HEAD
LONDON

RICHARD ATTENBOROUGH'S CRY FREEDOM

A PICTORIAL RECORD

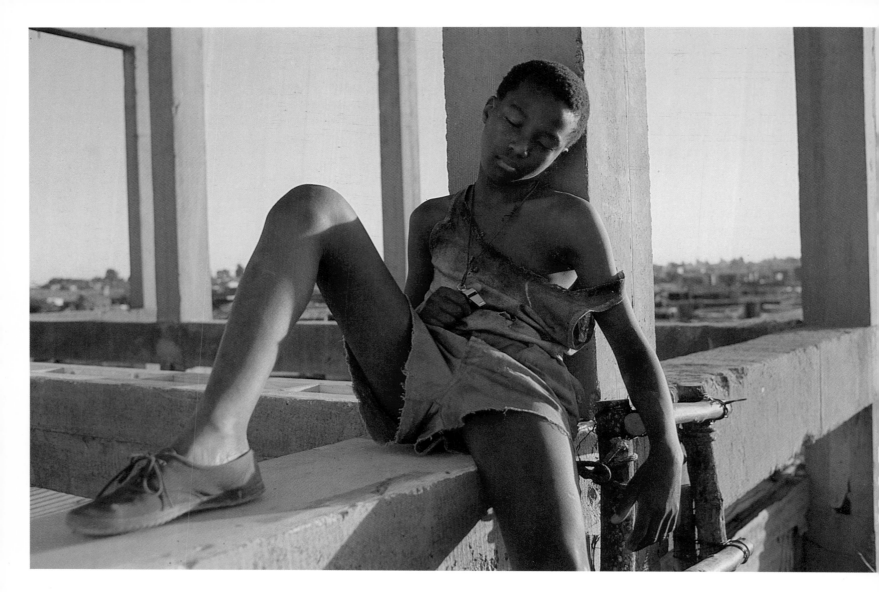

INTRODUCTION

I don't suppose many would consider *God is a Bad Policeman* the most exciting movie title of all time. However, in the late 1950s – even before I'd contemplated the possibility of a film on Mahatma Gandhi – I was working on a screenplay of that name dealing with apartheid.

I come from a radical family and, although I left home in Leicester to study at the Royal Academy of Dramatic Art in London at the age of seventeen, my formative years left an indelible impression. Any kind of racial or religious intolerance was anathema to my parents. This was graphically demonstrated to my brothers and me by their involvement in bringing Basque refugee children out of Spain during the Civil War and persecuted Jewish families out of Germany under Hitler's tyranny. The thought, therefore, that a nation could, in its parliament, enact laws which relegated one section of the community to an inferior position in perpetuity seemed to me not only inconceivable but obscene.

When I first went into production partnered by Bryan Forbes in 1959 to make a film called *The Angry Silence*, I think I already knew that if ever I was to direct – as against being a producer or an actor – the subject matter would essentially have to deal with social circumstances, and preferably in biographical terms since that is the kind of reading I most enjoy.

When it came to making the film of Gandhi's life in 1980, my colleagues and I had many discussions as to whether we should or could film the early part in South Africa where the Mahatma lived for over twenty years. Ultimately it proved impractical since the cost of taking an entire unit there from India was prohibitive and, anyway, most of the appropriate architecture existed in the sub-continent. For these reasons, and as there was an enormous amount of research material available, there seemed no point in my going to South Africa at that time. Those who did go were members of the Art Department, who had to re-create in India the look of that country at the turn of the century.

So it wasn't until the completion of *Gandhi* that I again contemplated visiting South Africa. While the current administration is in control, there is no question of *Cry Freedom* ever being shown there, but *Gandhi* was a different matter. The South Africans were prepared to permit the film to be distributed throughout the country, as a piece of history. Needless to say, there was no doubt in my mind that it should be shown before desegregated audiences. Initial discussions took place with Ster Kinekor, the film's local distributors, and they attempted, I believe in good faith, to obtain government assurances on this point. Then in 1983, on the day after we had received the bundle of Oscars for *Gandhi*, I was telephoned in Los Angeles by the London *Daily Mail* asking if it was true I intended to be present at a charity première held before an all-white audience. Naturally, I said that it was not.

We landed at London Airport to be told there was a large press contingent awaiting us. I suppose, with my actor's ego well to the fore, I assumed that they were assembled to ask about the success of a British film at the American Academy Awards. I couldn't have been more wrong.

Brushing aside the Oscars, their sole interest was in South Africa: whether or not I would be going there and if so under what circumstances. I did not do very well at the press conference. We'd flown all night and in any event I had not been to bed for a couple of days. I was, to say the least, inept, and what followed was not only extremely complex but also rather unpleasant.

Correspondence ensued between Ster Kinekor and myself. On 15 April 1983, in the South African Parliament, the Minister for Community Development stated he would make it possible for any *premières* (my italics) of the film to take place on a totally integrated racial basis throughout the Republic. On the same day, believing this was a step in the right direction, I said I would go, attend one integrated première at Linasia just outside Johannesburg and add my voice to those attempting to persuade the government this basic right should be granted for every showing of the film throughout its entire run. Immediately, I was inundated with messages and representations, both from groups and from individuals, all united in their determination to end apartheid but diverging widely on the means by which this could be achieved.

I knew that the ultimate decision had to be a purely personal one. Was it more correct morally – and I'm talking about nearly five years ago – to go to South Africa and make plain my total opposition to the system, or should I stay right away, close the door? By going would I, even tacitly, be condoning the regime?

For seven years I had been chairman of the British trustees of a multi-racial school in Swaziland called Waterford Kamhlaba. The principal driving force behind the school's creation was an English-speaking South African named Christopher Newton-Thompson. He lived in Johannesburg and was a member of the Progressive Federal Party of Helen Suzman and Van Zyl Slabbert which sits in opposition to the Nationalist Party, undefeated since it instituted apartheid in 1948. I felt that his opinion and the advice he might obtain from people such as Beyers Naudé, the great Afrikaner opponent of apartheid, from Helen Suzman herself and possibly others, might help in my deliberations. I had long phone calls with both Helen and Beyers, neither of whom I had met at that time, but of whom I knew a great deal.

On balance, I think Helen alone would have persuaded me to go in that she believes the system must be changed from within. She is an exceptional woman. For many years, single-handedly in the South African Parliament, she unceasingly opposed apartheid, suffering both abuse and humiliation in consequence. By contrast, Beyers, who had recently been Banned, ultimately came down on the side of staying away, saying he simply didn't trust the government to keep its word. Beyers believed that if I went, the authorities would somehow or another turn my acceptance to their advantage and that, however hard I tried, no matter what precautions I took, the final implication would be that I was prepared to condone segregation in the cinema.

Although largely persuaded by Beyers's advocacy, I delayed making my final decision for some days. I felt that nothing must place the distribution of the film in jeopardy but I wanted to make one last attempt to obtain desegregated screenings. By now I was under considerable pressure from the London Committee of the African National Congress. They maintained that to allow any showing whatsoever of the film in South Africa was a mistake and any question of my going would receive the unequivocal condemnation of the ANC throughout the world. Meanwhile, I was attacked in the South African Parliament for going back on my word. I had failed to accept the government's assurances, they said. I had at one time said I would go and then said I wouldn't. Finally, since the South African authorities had chosen to debate this whole matter in the public forum, on 18 April I issued a statement saying I would go if they would open every performance of *Gandhi* to all races throughout the film's entire run without requirement for any cinema to apply for a special permit. This challenge went unanswered.

Since delivering *Gandhi* to Columbia Pictures for worldwide distribution, I had been talking to my friend and manager, Marti Baum, a senior partner at CAA, the prestigious Los Angeles talent agency, about what I should do next. He believed that, rather than immediately tackling another film of social significance, I should look at other alternatives. He suggested a revolutionary idea – and one which by no means received universal approval – that I should direct a film of *A Chorus Line*, the longest-running musical in the history of theatre. After discussions with producers Cy Feuer and Ernie Martin, the doyens of Broadway theatre impresarios, I decided eventually that this was what I should do.

After making this decision, I was sent two books by their author, the exiled South African newspaper editor Donald Woods. I knew of him by reputation but had read neither *Biko* nor his autobiography, *Asking for Trouble*. Donald was suggesting I might like to make a film based on a combination of both.

Having read them, I was persuaded of their film potential and so we met. Donald brought with him Norman Spencer, a mutual friend, who had been his confidant for some time and who was to become the co-producer.

To me, one of the major problems in making a film about South Africa was that constantly changing circumstances could quickly render it utterly out of date. Also I didn't wish to make a film of despair. In one way Steve Biko's life, ending as and when it did, followed by a sham inquest only held due to pressure – largely from Donald – was a tragedy. Nothing could alter the appalling fact that one of the brightest, most charismatic, intelligent and fascinating men ever born in South Africa was murdered whilst in police custody. But what had developed, due to the publication of Donald's book, was that Steve's life became an inspirational rallying point for black people, not only in his country but throughout the whole of the African continent. In addition, Steve had demonstrated that black and white could live together in harmony once blacks were granted their rightful place in society. This, in simplistic form, was the fundamental credo of the Black Consciousness Movement: that black people should stand on their own feet in the belief that they were capable of anything whites could achieve and, as that belief grew, so too would their opportunities to fulfil those aspirations.

Donald had set this out most graphically and I saw that all the tenuous and rather vague thoughts I'd had about a film dealing with apartheid might perhaps be realised. *God is a Bad Policeman* had not been the only South African subject I'd optioned – there had been a number of others – but, in one way or another, all had failed to keep pace with the rapidly changing South African situation. Also I believed passionately that one must send an audience out of the theatre believing disaster is not inevitable. I wanted any anti-apartheid film I made to be unequivocal in its condemnation. But it still had to demonstrate that a solution was possible.

I told Donald and Norman I would attempt to find backing for the film. I knew it wouldn't be easy. Film financiers, in the main, are nervous of any subject of real substance. They are convinced that audiences around the world wish only to be "entertained" and that anything which challenges their views or engages their intelligence as well as their hearts is a potentially dangerous box office proposition. However, I recalled *Gandhi*. The man who had taken a chance and bought it was Frank Price, at that time head of Columbia Pictures, who had just been appointed to the equivalent position at Universal. I was on my way to Calgary to address an organisation honouring Lord Mountbatten of Burma when I read of Frank's move. I rang him on a Friday and he said he was moving in on the Monday morning. Why didn't I come then? It would be his first meeting as head of the new studios. I accepted at once.

When I arrived, we exchanged the usual pleasantries and he asked about my plans. "Well, Frank," I said, "I've got a subject which is bound to be as difficult as *Gandhi*. I want to make a film about South Africa. It's based on two books written by the exiled newspaper editor, Donald Woods."

"I know them well," he said. Apparently the late Carl Foreman had attempted on a number of occasions to persuade Columbia to make the picture, but for various reasons it had never materialised. "Do you have the screen rights now?"

When I replied that I had, Frank said he would be very content to finance a script and the necessary "recces" in order to see what the potential budget might be. "If it all works out satisfactorily we'll make it here at Universal," he said.

I returned to England in triumph. Donald and Norman were ecstatic. I had no doubt whatsoever as to who should write the script. Whatever success *Gandhi* achieved emanated in no small measure from Jack Briley's screenplay. I sent him Donald's books, we met and the film was under way.

A Chorus Line was completed and opened in America to reviews that were hardly unanimously eulogistic, but it did quite well worldwide and was an experience I would not have missed. It was a terrific challenge and technically is probably the best film I've ever made.

Now the question was whether, at last, I should go to South Africa. Since *Cry Freedom* was to deal with events which had happened only ten years earlier, it seemed to me that this was vital. I also believed it was essential to meet the current leaders of the black struggle, together with the men and women who had been Steve Biko's colleagues. But, most important of all, I felt that if I were to proceed with the film in the form in which it was developing, with Biko as the pivotal figure, I had to meet his widow, Ntsiki. Obviously we must seek her overall agreement.

For a long time I had longed to go to Waterford Kamhlaba in Swaziland. I was totally wedded to its concept of multi-racial education, but sadly had never seen the school at first hand. So the plan was that Sheila, my wife, and I would fly to Manzini. We decided not to go via Johannesburg as we didn't want to invoke the usual circus that tends to surround people in show business – particularly if they are concerned with controversial matters.

We had a marvellous few days at Waterford, although we were plagued with the worst rainstorms that anybody could remember. As a result, on our departure we had to wade across the river at the bottom of the hill on which the school stands, with a number of the boy pupils carrying our luggage on their heads – an absurd image which always makes me laugh whenever I think back. We then embarked on the drive to the South African border with Christopher Newton-Thompson and his wife Philippa. All seemed perfectly straightforward at the frontier. We produced our passports and I felt that they were taken, examined and handed back quite routinely. However, Sheila thought she heard one of the border guards mention our name within an Afrikaans sentence. She may have been right and subsequent events showed she probably was, because it turned out that we were observed from that time on.

We entered South Africa on 30 January 1984 and stayed with the Newton-Thompsons for three days. Philippa took us into Soweto and she and Christopher arranged for us to meet a number of remarkable people while we were there. We then flew to Cape Town where hotel rooms had been reserved under a pseudonym, again so that we wouldn't be pestered by the press. On arrival we handed over our passports in the normal way and consequently the hotel was fully aware of our real identity. That night we had dinner with Helen Suzman. It was a

joy to meet this courageous woman I had only previously known as a voice on the telephone. Next day we visited Khayelitsha, destined to become the transit camp to which those dispossessed by the destruction of Crossroads would be sent. It was a massive construction at the end of a giant double carriageway in the middle of the desert, and chillingly reminiscent of the labour camps in Germany before World War II. Over lunch we met Donald's friend Tony Heard, editor of the *Cape Times*, and also Van Zyl Slabbert, then leader of the Progressive Federal Party who, nearly two years later, would resign to fight apartheid from outside Parliament. After lunch, on the way to our room, Sheila and I were buttonholed by a young Afrikaner reporter who asked a number of questions including, surprisingly, whether we were in South Africa to make arrangements for a film on the life of Steve Biko. I was able to say it was a private visit and were there to be a film, it would not be purely about the life of Biko.

The following morning we were to leave for the Wild Coast to meet other friends and colleagues of Donald. As we emerged from our bedroom at 6.30 a.m., there outside our door, emblazoned in the boldest type possible on the front page of the Afrikaans paper *Die Burger*, was a headline: *ATTENBOROUGH IN KAAPSTAD*. Whatever cover we thought we had was certainly blown.

We spent three happy and relaxing days on the Wild Coast, returning to East London with Don Card, a staunch friend of Donald who, until he could no longer tolerate their methods, had been a member of the security police. Now, in the Eastern Cape, came the most important element of our entire journey: the meeting with Steve Biko's widow, Ntsiki.

First, however, we were to go to King William's Town and visit the Zanempilo Clinic which had been founded and run by the Black Consciousness Movement. This was a fairly simple trip which provided a wonderful insight into the scale and ingenuity of their whole operation.

I would hardly describe our visit to Ntsiki as simple, though. It was like a le Carré novel. We had to change cars several times and go in and out of various buildings and hotels, in at the back door and out of the front, in at the front door and out of

With Ntsiki Biko (*Photograph Sheila Attenborough*)

the back, with sometimes a car following us, sometimes our following a car. The other car's occupant was Ntsiki, accompanied, as it turned out, by her mother-in-law. Eventually we arrived undetected at the Amatola Sun Hotel in Zwelitsha, which had an ambience as inappropriate as one could possibly imagine, with a garish superficial gloss of wealth that was the very antithesis of everything the Biko family stood for.

Both women were enchanting: gracious, kind, and greatly interested in what we had to say. I explained as graphically as I could the situation about a possible film. I made it plain that in no way were we contemplating a biography of Steve, that the basis of the potential screenplay would be Donald's two books and that Steve's involvement, although probably pivotal, would be in the context of two families rather than one. I came to the end and there was a pause. Ntsiki asked if she might talk to her mother-in-law for a few moments in Xhosa because Mrs Biko senior spoke virtually no English. After a little while, they turned to Sheila and me again. "We would like you to try and make your film," Ntsiki said. "We would like you to make it for two

reasons. Firstly because you have taken the trouble to come and see us and ask our opinion, and secondly because Donald was one of Steve's very closest friends."

I felt that we could not possibly have asked for more and we left knowing that, should the film go ahead, we at least had the approval in principle of the most important living figure apart from Donald and Wendy Woods.

From East London, we flew to Durban to fulfil my long-term quest and meet the South African branch of Mahatma Gandhi's family. Like all Indians, their hospitality knew no bounds and our meeting – though tearful – was immensely joyful. Through reminiscence and a mass of anecdotes they filled in all sorts of missing details about Gandhi's life and those of his sons which I found fascinating.

From Durban we flew to Bloemfontein to meet Winnie Mandela, who lived some sixty or seventy kms north at Brandfort. Since our brief encounter with the young reporter in Cape Town, we had seen nothing more of the press. The arrival at Bloemfontein Airport was, however, somewhat different. Waiting for us were twenty or thirty reporters and photographers and two television crews. The manager of the local hotel fortunately managed to whisk us away and, as a result, we were left in peace during the evening. At crack of dawn the following morning, in a self-drive car, we left for Brandfort, arriving early at the post office car park where, by pre-arrangement, we were to meet Mrs Mandela. She arrived on time in her beige Volkswagen minibus and strode towards us like an empress in a flowing purple gown. It was well understood that we could meet her only one at a time since she was the subject of a Banning Order.

I got out of the car and went towards her. Although we'd been aware of two security police vehicles which had pulled up since our arrival, we were taken aback when, like a genie out of a lamp, a television crew from the South African Broadcasting Corporation also appeared. They filmed our initial meeting and, when we arrived eventually at Winnie's little house in the black township, they were still in attendance. Winnie lived in two rooms, each about ten feet square. I went in first while Sheila waited outside. I emerged after about an hour and the SABC crew filmed Winnie answering a few questions. Then their reporter, Freek Swart, asked me for an interview. At first I was very reluctant, but I was persuaded when he pointed out that, as Winnie had been particularly gracious about us, it would be discourteous if I didn't say a few words in return. After the interview had been completed, the SABC crew disappeared. Sheila and I spent two further hours with Winnie, talking about her own position, the general situation in South Africa and the circumstances of her visits to her famous husband, Nelson Mandela, who at that time was imprisoned on Robben Island. Finally we left.

We returned to Bloemfontein Airport. One or two of the press were still there, but there was nothing like the mass of journalists that had previously descended upon us. We arrived back in Johannesburg to be met by yet more friends of Donald

With Winnie Mandela (*Photograph Sheila Attenborough*)

and Wendy who drove us to Pretoria, telling us we were to appear on television that night. Little did we imagine what was in store when, later, we all settled down to watch the news.

I was accused of asking Mrs Mandela for secret addresses where documents could be sent from London. Even more ridiculously, Swart said I'd enquired whether, under certain circumstances, Xhosas would be prepared to associate themselves with terrorists who, it was alleged, I'd called "freedom fighters". The audience was also told I was planning a film to improve the image of the African National Congress overseas and this would be finished by Christmas, with its release timed to coincide with protests and strikes throughout South Africa.

Sheila and I were both speechless – not only because of the attention devoted to our visit to Winnie, but also because of the quite extraordinary distortion and dishonesty which permeated almost every sentence that Swart uttered. I should have known better, of course. Since Winnie was Banned, she could not be quoted in the press or on television, and yet Swart had filmed an interview with her, supposedly for transmission, before asking me to appear. It was of course a ruse which I should have seen through at once. Naively, however, I didn't, and from then on the authorities and, I fear, a considerable number of other white South Africans were determined we should leave the country.

This became evident the following day when we drove some 250 kms north to meet one of Steve's colleagues, Dr Mamphela Ramphele, another outstanding figure in the history of the black struggle in South Africa. Returning from the Ithuseng Community Health Centre which she had established almost single-handedly in Zaneen, we stopped at a petrol station. Sheila and our girl driver went into the ladies' lavatory and I went to the gents'. As we pulled up, so had a Range Rover full of young, slightly drunk white South Africans who'd obviously been on a fishing or hunting trip. They followed me into the lavatory and, when I went to leave, barred the door. I don't know whether they spoke English or not, but they chose to address me in Afrikaans. It was, however, very evident from a combination of their attitude and the frequent mention of Winnie Mandela's name that they were enraged by the television report which they had obviously seen the previous evening. I have to admit that, for a few moments, I was really quite frightened. I thought they might knock me about, but because they were by no means sober I managed with some fast footwork to get out. They followed me to the car where our Afrikaans-speaking driver confirmed my worst suspicions. Their language was disgusting, and the insinuations they were making about Winnie and myself unbelievably crude.

The following day we were closely shadowed all the way to the airport. I must say I have rarely felt happier to board a British Airways plane and to know we were safely on our way home.

On the journey I found it unusually difficult to sleep, so vivid were the images engraved on my mind – images of courage, compassion, despair and, needless to say, of belligerence. I remembered so clearly eight or ten of the people I had met who, for their own safety, must here remain anonymous. I remembered also Dr Motlana, the leading black spokesman in Soweto, Mamphela Ramphele, Ntsiki Biko, her mother-in-law and, as much as anyone, the heroic Beyers Naudé whom we had met only hours earlier. His face remains clearly in my mind's eye: a bespectacled man of medium height who would be, I suppose, in his middle sixties, with that extraordinary, in some instances unattractive, South African speech pattern, a man of such compassion and forgiveness that he must take his place ultimately as one of the most significant men in the whole of African history. His intellect, his analytical powers, his objective yet tolerant attitudes were profoundly impressive and I shall always consider myself fortunate indeed to have met him.

All that I'd seen and heard confirmed my determination to make the movie. We could, I believed, contain the subject matter within a precise period of time and yet encapsulate all that was currently of such burning importance in attempting to analyse and understand the position in South Africa. The story was, although relatively recent history, just sufficiently removed from contemporary circumstances to permit a measure of objectivity, however small that might be.

Jack Briley started to work on the actual screenplay. In the end I think there were some nine amended versions, with one or two fundamental changes of concept being thrown up during the writing period. We had numerous conferences and eventually were joined, hour after hour, day after day, by Donald, Wendy and Norman Spencer until we had agreed upon the final script. As far as Donald and Wendy were concerned, it was a process that, I suspect, was personally both cathartic and painful, complicated by their evident sense of responsibility in terms of political and historical authenticity.

Donald and Wendy Woods are two of the most courageous people I have ever met. They are both, in the truest sense of the word, extraordinary. Their life, before they encountered Steve Biko, was that of most fairly affluent English-speaking white South Africans. They lived in a spacious, architect-designed house with a private swimming pool, ran two cars and had a live-in black maid called Evalina whom they and their children adored. Donald played golf regularly. Wendy, an excellent pianist, gave her spare time to various charitable activities. Their social standing in East London on the Eastern Cape was high, despite the fact that Donald, through his editorship of the *Daily Dispatch*, was a well-known opponent of apartheid. Then they met Steve Biko and espoused the cause of Black Consciousness. When Steve was murdered in security police detention, Donald campaigned so vigorously for an inquest he was declared a Banned Person and the family was subjected to a campaign of intimidation by the same security police. At that point, I think, with so much to lose, most ordinary people would have quietly jettisoned their moral convictions. What makes the Woods extraordinary is that they did not, that they were prepared to sacrifice their comfortable lifestyle, abandon everything they had built up over the years and, with five children, make a new start in a different country in order that Steve's story could be made known to the world. *Cry Freedom* is part of Donald and Wendy's continuing crusade against apartheid. It is also, largely, their story, and our script conferences obliged them, a decade later, to revive many traumatic memories and re-open old wounds.

Donald and Wendy Woods.

Trips to Los Angeles eventually resulted in overall approval of the screenplay, although Frank Price accepted that, principally in the flash-back concept and the refining of dialogue, I still wished to make a number of modifications.

Concurrently, other vital groundwork – the film's budget and the schedule on which it is based – was being undertaken elsewhere. This was in the hands of my long-standing executive producer, colleague and partner, Terry Clegg, and John Trehy, who is probably the best financial controller in the British film industry. A schedule is largely based on the findings and conclusions of the production designer and I was happy that Stuart Craig, who had worked on both *A Bridge Too Far* and *Gandhi*, was also able to join us. Terry had just finished work on *Out of Africa* and therefore favoured shooting in Kenya. However, for topographical and other reasons – mainly architectural similarities – we ultimately chose Zimbabwe.

In the choice of location everything depends upon the willingness and capability of the authorities to accommodate an enterprise on the scale of a $20 million picture. In Harare we were fortunate enough to find, in the person of Mrs Beverley Tilly, a government official of whom I can say categorically that the picture would never have been made there without her. She works for a remarkable man, Dr Nathan Shamuyarira, the Minister of Information, Posts and Telecommunications, and, once they had read the script, without any requests for revisions, they gave us the go-ahead. Under the authority of its indefatigable chief executive, Charles Ndhlovu, the ministry's Central Film Laboratories – in addition to the facilities they granted us locally – invested in the film some 18% of its total budget. Through ZANU PF, the majority party in Zimbabwe, we were given enormous assistance in that police and army alike were put at our disposal whenever we asked for them. Roads were closed, buildings were set aside for our use, every form of transport was made available and, in terms of gathering the vast crowds that we needed for the re-enactment of Steve Biko's funeral and for the massacre at Soweto, the party's infrastructure was invaluable.

It had always been my intention to cast one of the black African actors who, for various reasons, are spread around the world to play Steve Biko. In fact, I interviewed between ninety-five and a hundred of them for the part. It was an extraordinarily difficult role to cast, particularly as Steve is very clear in modern memory and had a number of distinctive attributes. He was over six feet tall, very good looking, intelligent, dynamic and as charismatic as any major movie star. He had the ability in his relaxed manner to capture and hold an audience – be it twenty people in a room or a thousand in an assembly hall – with consummate ease. I saw more and more actors and became increasingly depressed as the possibility of finding someone from Southern Africa receded. We looked all over the world. Despite the difference in physiognomy, I even began to consider West Indians. Finally I decided that, since the part also required immense acting skills, the search must expand to include the United States.

A number of the superb black American actors who have emerged during the past five or ten years were very anxious to play Steve and I met several of them. However, the one who really attracted my attention, in a totally different part, was

Denzel Washington. I had seen him in *A Soldier's Story* and although his characterisation and appearance in that film were in no way comparable to Steve Biko, I felt he was an actor of great depth and skill, coupled with what I can only describe as star quality. He was kind enough to come to see me at the Regency Hotel in New York, having flown in from Houston. I talked to him about the film's subject, of which he didn't know a great deal, and, as he thought about the sort of man he was being asked to play, he came alive, he glowed. I felt that if I failed in my search for an African, Denzel was a very real possibility.

We tested a number of actors, professional and amateur alike. But it was no good. They simply weren't right. So I watched *A Soldier's Story* yet again and also *St Elsewhere*, the television series in which Denzel appears. Finally, having abandoned all hope of finding an African and without even testing him because I felt so certain of his ability, I offered Denzel the part.

Casting Donald was somewhat easier although once more I had to find a man of particular physique and personality, this time in his late thirties or early forties. A number of British actors discussed the part with me, but I never felt that they were completely right, and obviously the film's success depended on the chemistry between the two leading men. An actor I'd had in mind for some time was Kevin Kline. Physically he was ideal. I'd seen him in several films and admired him greatly – particularly in *Sophie's Choice*. I was very anxious to see his *Hamlet* in New York and having watched his performance, I had no doubt that he was the right man for the part. My only concern was the accent. But I needn't have worried, either in his case or Denzel's. The extraordinary accuracy of their South African speech patterns will earn both of them the admiration of anyone who knows just how difficult it is to reproduce that particular sound and cadence.

I had always hoped Wendy would be played by Penelope Wilton, but unfortunately she was committed to the National Theatre and I started to look for someone else. I'd met Penelope – Pep – in the waiting room of my dentist in Upper Wimpole Street. It wasn't the conventional way in which director should meet actress but it was enough.

Susie Figgis, our casting director, whose contribution to the picture was very considerable indeed – particularly in our search for black actors and actresses – assembled a number of very interesting players. But, despite some excellent tests, I was looking for a highly individual personality and no one proved ideal. I still hoped that something would change and Pep might be free. My hopes were, in fact, answered when the arrangement she had with the National fell through and, after a brief camera test, I was confirmed in my view that we'd found the perfect Wendy.

We have, I believe, a terrific line-up of actors and actresses, and many are South African expatriates giving performances which have a great deal more personal significance than merely filling a particular role.

So finally *Cry Freedom* went into production. We shot for just over twelve weeks in Zimbabwe, two days in Kenya and finished with four weeks' studio work at Shepperton in England. That we completed the picture on time and under budget is due, in no small measure, to the unique skills of David Tomblin, who is undoubtedly the world's finest first assistant director, and to Ronnie Taylor and Eddie Collins, respectively director of photography and camera operator.

The new member of the principal team on this picture is our editor, Lesley Walker. Her sympathy for the subject, together with her undoubted skills, made working with her a total joy.

Finally, of course, came the music. Remembering his work on *Gandhi*, I decided it should be entrusted to George Fenton, whose talent – not only as a musician but also in terms of understanding what music can contribute to cinema – is probably without equal. He and his African collaborator, Jonas Gwangwa, have, I believe, created a distinguished score.

After nine months of editing and dubbing at Twickenham Studios near London, we delivered the completed film to Universal. Frank Price is no longer with the company, although the head of production, Sean Daniel, still remains. He, together with Frank's successor, Tom Pollock, and MCA president Sid

Sheinberg have continued to give me every possible support in completing the production.

This book contains over a hundred and thirty colour photographs, most of which were taken by Frank Connor, aided and abetted by Simon Mein and Jody Boulting. They will, I hope, capture not only the film's story but also the atmosphere and magic of that part of the African continent in which we worked.

Zimbabwe is the most beautiful country, with a warmth of hospitality which is quite bewildering when one considers that the civil war in which they were cruelly involved ended only in 1980. Anyone who doubts the ultimate viability of a multi-racial society should spend time in Zimbabwe. It seems to me that what they have achieved in a very short space of time under the leadership of their Prime Minister, Robert Mugabe, is little short of miraculous. The people and government gave us every possible help and I hope that this film's very existence becomes part of their protest against apartheid.

Eventually I'm certain a solution will be found to the current tragedy that engulfs South Africa. There will inevitably be different factions, determined on particular courses and each convinced that their way provides the only hope. The answer is, of course, far more complex than merely sanctions or no sanctions, violence or no violence. However, there is evidently one vital element now being brought to bear on the situation – both in Africa and the rest of the world – and that is a ground swell of revulsion against the whole concept of apartheid, against the whole idea that one human being is superior to another human being. In the end, right will prevail. I can only hope, as do my colleagues and, I know, all those who helped us so significantly in Zimbabwe, that this film might in some small measure help to sway world opinion and so hasten the day when all Africans will be free.

Amandla!

RICHARD ATTENBOROUGH

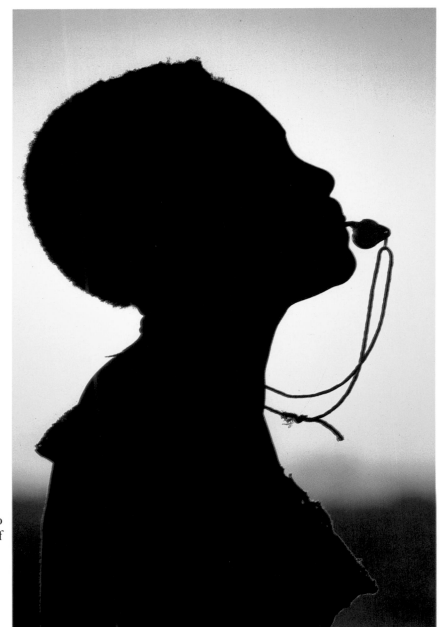

Children, acting as lookouts, use whistles to warn illegal black squatter communities of impending police raids.

Crossroads, an area occupied by illegal squatters in Cape Province, South Africa. At dawn in November 1975, police storm into the shanty township behind a "sneeze machine" belching tear gas.

The raiders use vicious dogs and sjamboks – official-issue whips – to round up men, women and children.

Those without the requisite Pass will be transported to transit camps, fenced with barbed wire, where many – particularly the children – will succumb to disease or malnutrition before they can be sent on to remote, barren tribal Homelands.

After the raid, the settlement is systematically bulldozed and burnt until only rubble and desolation remain. But gradually, defiant in their stoicism, those who escaped arrest return to salvage what they can and, before nightfall, rebuild some kind of shelter.

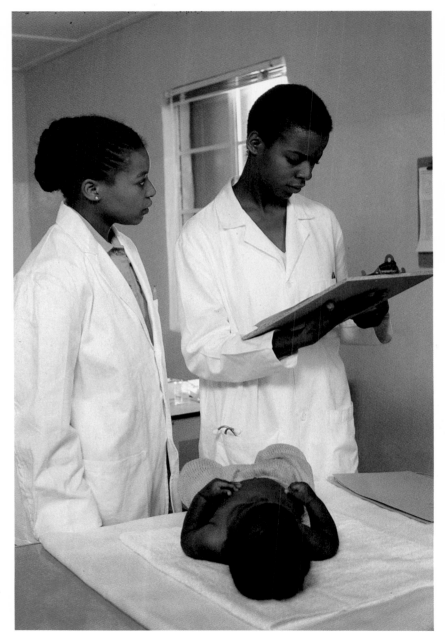

At Zanempilo Clinic, Dr Mamphela Ramphele has heard of the raid on state radio. Tenjy Mtintso, helping her with morning rounds, fears that Steve Biko, a young civil rights activist and one of the clinic's founders, may be one of those arrested. But, over breakfast, Steve's wife, Ntsiki, is calmly confident they would have been alerted had he fallen into police hands.

Donald Woods, editor of the *Daily Dispatch* in East London, prints photographs of atrocities committed during the raid as part of his paper's continuing crusade against apartheid. At the same time, he attacks as equally racist the policies of Steve Biko's Black Consciousness Movement from which white liberals – such as himself – are specifically excluded.

Accustomed, like most white South Africans, to blacks who are servile and self-effacing, Woods is taken aback when his editorial results in angry confrontation with Dr Ramphele who challenges him to meet Steve Biko and discover the truth for himself.

Biko lives in King William's Town. At a church, converted by local blacks into a thriving community centre, Woods is greeted by the young activist's wife.

A garden shed, set apart from the church, serves as the 28-year-old Biko's office. Declared a Banned Person, he is forbidden to be with more than one person at a time and, in addition to many other restrictions, is under constant official surveillance. After some verbal sparring which reveals that both men have a sense of humour, Biko offers Woods his hand. This simple gesture is the basis for a friendship which will transcend age, race, custom – even death – and change the entire course of the journalist's life.

Plain-clothes security police, who believe they follow Biko everywhere, tail Woods's Mercedes on a visit to Zanempilo. The self-supporting clinic, staffed entirely by blacks, explains Biko, cogently demonstrates to those who use it that medical and organisational skills are not the sole prerogative of whites. As their servants, doing every menial and underpaid job available, blacks know a great deal about the luxurious lifestyle of people like Woods. But they – even liberal, supposedly informed people such as he – know next to nothing about the living conditions of the other ninety per cent of South Africa's population.

While their five children play in the spacious garden of his secluded home and the family's live-in maid, Evalina, serves refreshments, Woods describes the surprisingly impressive Biko to his wife, Wendy.

Biko prepares to accompany Woods on an educational visit to a typical black township. Dr Ramphele and Ntsiki fear police will catch him outside King William's Town, his designated Banning Area.

Many youngsters living in the township are the children of live-in maids such as Evalina, only free to see them for a few hours once a week. That they survive at all in an environment of despair, drunkenness and thuggery, is, Biko says a miracle.

No matter how smart or dumb a black child may be this ghetto is where he must live and where, inevitably, he will die.

Transitory escape for the adult men, separated from their families, is to be found in shebeens providing music, alcohol and drugs.

Biko takes Woods to the township home of Tenjy's relatives who describe the caring tribal society in which black Africans lived before the arrival of the white man.

Now committed to Biko and to the cause of Black Consciousness, Woods employs Tenjy and Mapetla as journalists on the *Daily Dispatch*.

Woods takes Ken, one of his photographers, to a
football match where Biko and other black activists
are to make illegal speeches.

Woods and Ken are the only whites present.
Biko's address to the crowd clearly demonstrates the powerfully charismatic personality of a born leader, seeking to arm blacks not with hatred but with pride.

An informer in the pay of the security police, anonymity grotesquely enshrined in a large cardboard box, identifies Biko as having broken his Ban by speaking at the football match.

When Biko calmly refutes the informer's credibility as a witness, police hold him down while Captain de Wet, a long-standing and vicious adversary, smashes an open-handed blow into his face.

The moment his arms are freed, Biko returns the blow, bloodying de Wet's nose. Only an imminent appearance in court, where he has been subpoenaed as a witness, saves Biko from being beaten up. But de Wet threatens dire consequences should he ever fall into the hands of the security police again.

Biko is called as a witness at the trial of nine other Black Consciousness leaders. His disarming frankness and lucidity turn the tables on a white prosecutor attempting to trap him into damaging admissions concerning the aims of the movement.

A masked gang wreck the King William's Town
community centre.

When the masks are removed, a black night watchman
hiding in a tree recognises one of the gang as Captain
de Wet.

Suspecting that any protest lodged locally will be met with denial and inaction, Woods travels to the Pretoria home of Justice Minister, Jimmy Kruger. Having publicly vowed to eliminate police illegality,

Kruger listens sympathetically to Woods's complaint. He appears stunned by the disclosure that a black witness Woods refuses to name for fear of reprisals has positively identified de Wet.

Next morning in East London, two sinister security police visit the Woods's home. The senior man, Lemick, states they have orders "from the very top" to imprison Donald if he continues to withhold the name of the witness. Since Kruger alone has the necessary authority to approve such an order, Woods has to face the unpalatable truth that police corruption in South Africa extends from "the very top" down to the level of de Wet and his masked bully-boys.

Again breaking the terms of his Ban, Steve enjoys a
game of rugby with black friends.

Woods tracks Biko down to tell him that he has been summoned for failing to reveal the name of the witness. A few months in gaol, Biko teases, will do much to ensure the editor's credibility as a budding activist.

In the middle of the night, accompanied by two henchmen, Lemick goes to search Biko's township house for subversive literature. Steve opens the door, feigning amiable sleepiness.

He calmly requests Lemick to let him read the search warrant through a window and, shutting the door, wordlessly hands incriminating documents to Ntsiki who hides them in the baby's diaper.

Lemick is obliged to hold the warrant up to the light and allow Steve, very slowly and methodically, to read it from beginning to end.

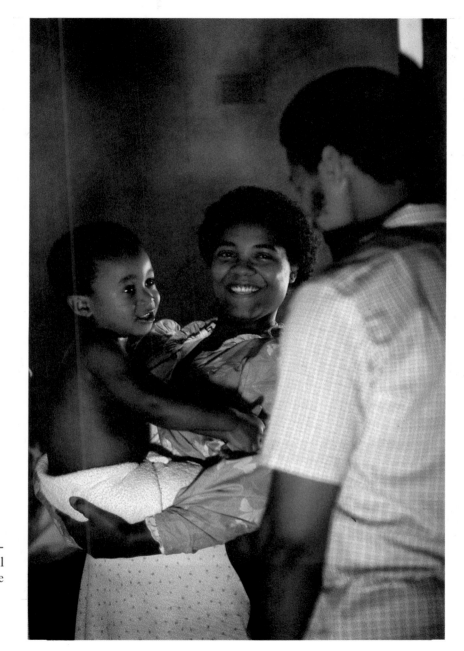

Steve finally allows the outmanoevred Lemick into their home for a search that will
prove fruitless and when he leaves even the
baby joins in the laughter.

Again late at night, police wake Evalina in her quarters at the Woods's house, demanding to inspect her Pass.

An outraged Donald, wildly brandishing a revolver,
orders the "intruders" off his premises.

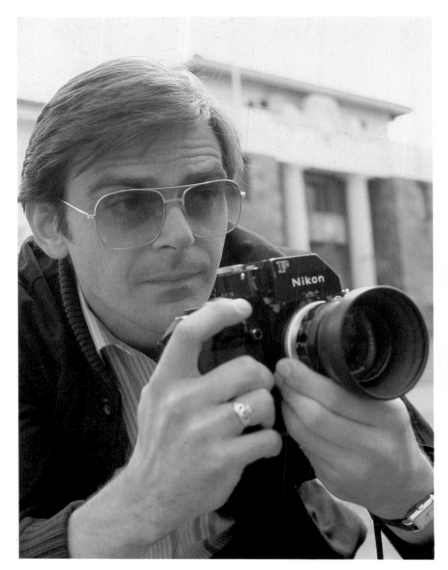

The authorities apply further pressure. Woods's
staff cameraman, Ken, photographs security police
snatching Mapetla outside the *Daily Dispatch* office.

On the night of Mapetla's arrest, Steve visits Donald and Wendy and tells them that soon he intends to travel far outside his Banning Area to address a students' meeting in Capetown.

Woods hears that Mapetla has died in security police
detention. The official explanation is that he hanged
himself in his cell.

Biko reveals that, prior to his "suicide", guards showed another detainee a puppet of Mapetla hanging from a string.

While driving Biko to Capetown, his friend and
colleague Peter Jones is flagged down at a roadblock.

Jones hands over his keys for a routine search but the police become suspicious and decide to investigate further. The car's passenger is ordered onto the roadside and forced to utter the name on his Pass, the name of a Banned Person forbidden to travel beyond the confines of faraway King William's Town, the name of the man most wanted by security police in all South Africa: Bantu Stephen Biko.

Twenty-four days later, a doctor is hastily summoned to Walmer Police Station in Port Elizabeth.

He finds Biko – face beaten to an almost unrecognizable pulp – lying naked, manacled and comatose on the cement floor of a cell.

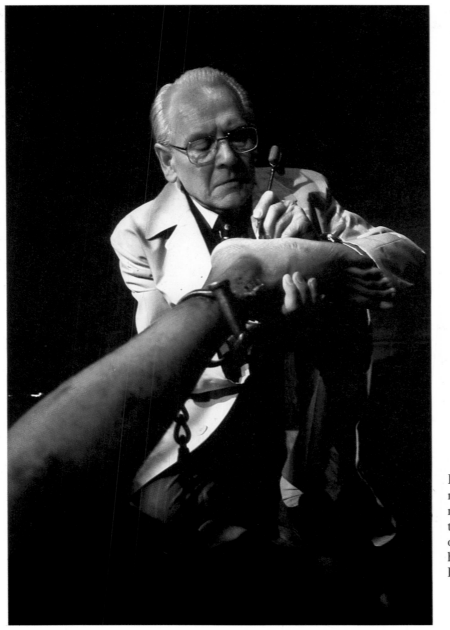

Biko's reflexes prove that he has sustained massive brain damage and requires urgent medical attention. Overriding weak protestations from the doctor, a senior police officer decrees he will be taken seven hundred miles to the police hospital in Pretoria.

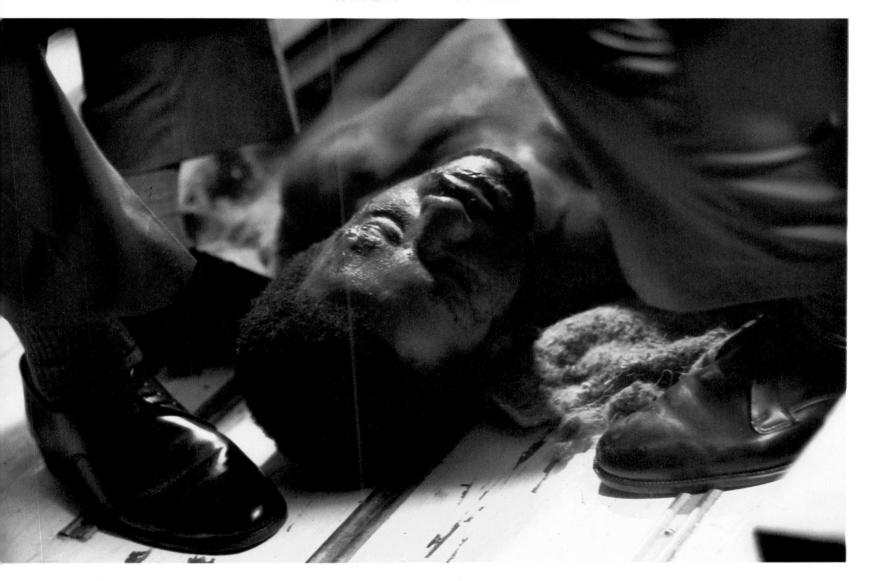

Still naked, Biko is thrown onto the floor of a Land Rover with only a thin mat to cushion his head from the jolting as it speeds through the night. He dies in Pretoria next day, 12 September 1977.

Dr Ramphele hears the news at Zanempilo Clinic.

Wendy Woods grieves in her East London garden.

In Biko's township house, Ntsiki and her two small
sons mourn a husband and a father.

"Biko's death leaves me cold. He died after a hunger strike," proclaims Justice Minister Kruger to a cheering audience at an Afrikaner Nationalist Party rally.

By pre-arrangement a short while later, Donald Woods meets Ntsiki Biko.

They drive, with Ken, to a segregated mortuary.

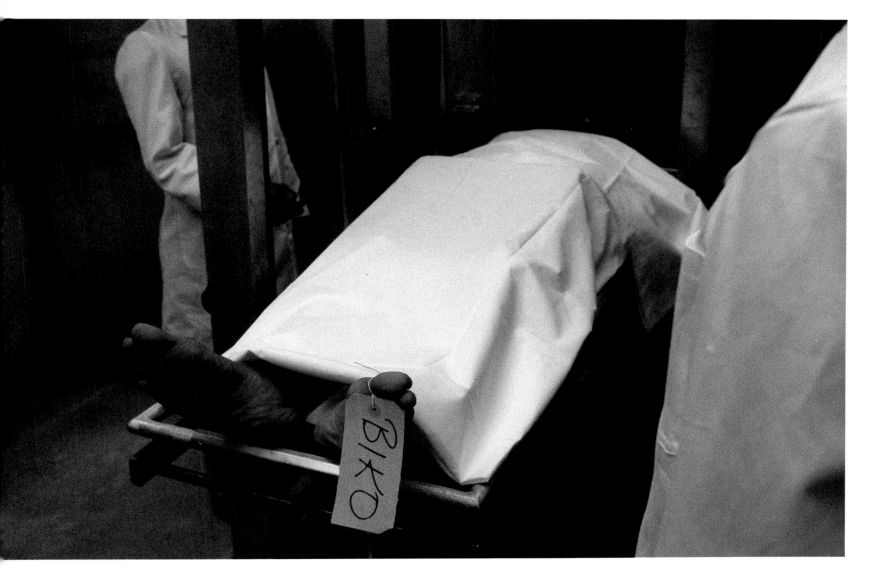

Woods, exercising Ntsiki's legal right as next of kin,
demands that she be allowed to see Steve's body.

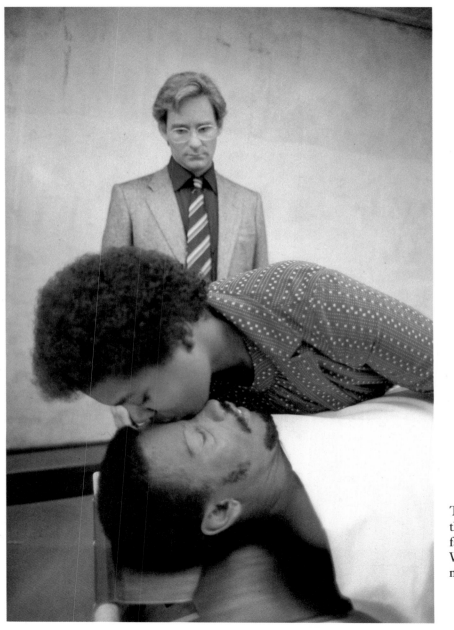

The battered corpse plainly demonstrates that Kruger's callous disclaimer is a blatant falsehood. In order to expose it as such, Woods instructs Ken to photograph Steve's multiple injuries from every possible angle.

Some twenty thousand mourners – the vast majority black – pay their last respects to Steve Biko. Many, many thousands more have been turned away by police.

Understandably, the initial mood at Biko's funeral is one of anger.

Many present brandish posters showing Steve breaking the manacles that symbolise the brutal oppression of his people.

Ntsiki and Steve's sons flanked by his mother and brother.

Amongst the few whites present, Donald and Wendy Woods.

(*Over page*) Hostility gives way to grief and hope for a better future as, led by a member of the Black Consciousness Movement, the massed mourners join in singing the dignified and moving cadences of the African Anthem: "God bless Africa. Raise up her spirit . . . Hear our prayers and bless us."

Late at night, while Kruger continues to imply that Biko starved himself to death, Wendy receives the latest in a series of threatening and obscene phone calls.

This time the callers act out their threat, firing shots at the house and daubing it with slogans denouncing the Woods as Communists. Don Card, a family friend and ex-member of the force himself, will prove with ballistics that the bullets came from guns issued to serving members of the security police.

Seeking international support for his campaign to force an official inquest into the cause of Steve's death, Donald attempts to leave the country. He is detained at the airport and learns that he, too, is now Banned. For the next five years, as was Steve, he is not allowed to be with more than one person at a time – other than members of his immediate family – to write anything, to be quoted by name in the media or to travel outside the magisterial district of his home in East London.

Disregarding constant security police surveillance, the bugging of his home and the conditions of his Ban which expressly forbid it, Donald now starts to write a book. The manuscript, which he keeps hidden, is a biography of Steve, intended to reveal – following a sham inquest which totally exonerated those responsible – how he met his death.

Donald's friend, Father Kani, warns that he must either destroy the manuscript or somehow get it, himself and his entire family out of South Africa.

At the beach, where they cannot be overheard, Donald presents Wendy with an ultimatum.

"What do you mean, we've got to leave?" is her angry response.

There is no writer, Donald explains, who knows Steve's story as he does and no way his story can be made known to the outside world unless the book is published abroad. The South African authorities will regard it as treason.

Wendy cannot come to terms with the idea of ripping the children from their home, their schools, their grandparents. In addition, she points out, they could take no money and would arrive at their destination penniless.

A parcel arrives at the Woods's house, addressed to the children. It contains little T-shirts bearing a picture of Steve.

Mary Woods, aged five, tries on the smallest T-shirt and starts to scream. Her face, hands and arms are blotched with acid burns.

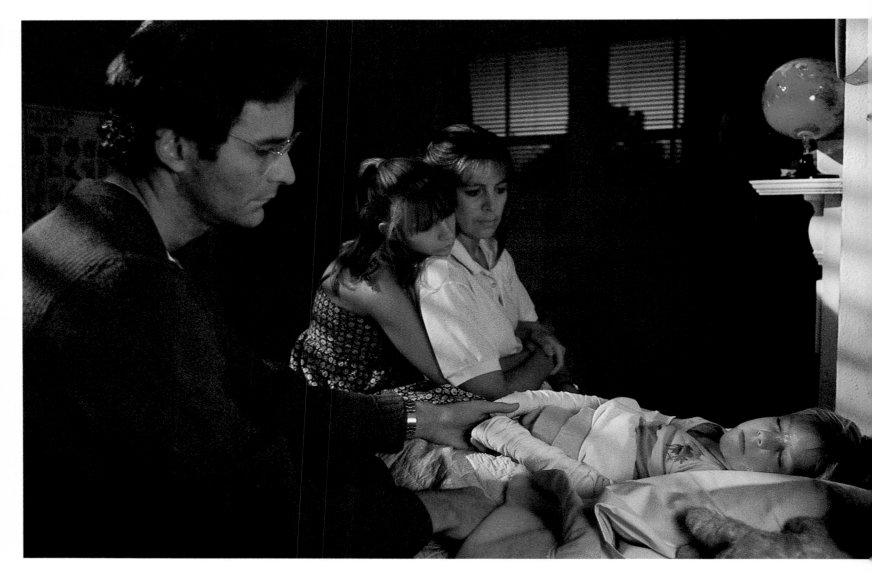

Don Card proves, yet again, that this is the handiwork of the security police. Mary will make a full recovery but Wendy now accepts that Donald is right. They must leave.

Bruce, an Australian journalist friend, helps to hatch an escape plan. On New Year's Eve, Donald will attempt to cross the South African border into Lesotho and, once he is safe, Wendy and the children will follow.

To conform with the photograph in a "borrowed" passport, Donald dyes his hair and will travel disguised as a priest.

Although Evalina and the younger Woods children are kept in ignorance of the plan, teenage Jane is fully aware of the danger.

Wendy smuggles Donald past watching security
police in the family Mercedes.

For the first and longest stage of his 400-mile
journey Donald is to hitch hike.

In East London, still under close surveillance and with concealed microphones everywhere, Wendy maintains the pretence that he has never left the house.

Dawn. Donald has less than five hours to reach his destination and make the prearranged phone call that will start Wendy on her journey. But, after heavy recent rain, the Telle River is in full flood. Not wanting to further implicate Father Kani, Donald decides to continue alone. Intent on keeping the manuscript of his precious biography dry at all costs, he attempts to ford the river – and fails.

Donald finds refuge and a place to dry his clothes with jovial Tami and his family.

Imagining the government's embarrassment when Woods escapes and the biography is published makes Tami roar with laughter.

Donald has decided to try and bluff his way into
Lesotho using the "borrowed" passport, and Tami
drives him to a point above the border post.

He now has only three hours to reach Maseru,
capital of Lesotho, and make the call to Wendy.

A postal official, aptly named Moses, offers Woods a
lift across the frontier.

In East London, after a long, anxious night, Wendy pretends for the benefit of the younger children they are going on a picnic. For her own protection, Evalina cannot be told the truth either. This means, when the moment comes to leave their home for the last time, there are no farewells.

Moses drives across the bridge spanning the Telle
River and into Lesotho.

Donald celebrates his freedom with a tribal dance.
Now, in spite of appalling road conditions, it is up to
Bruce to get him to Maseru on time.

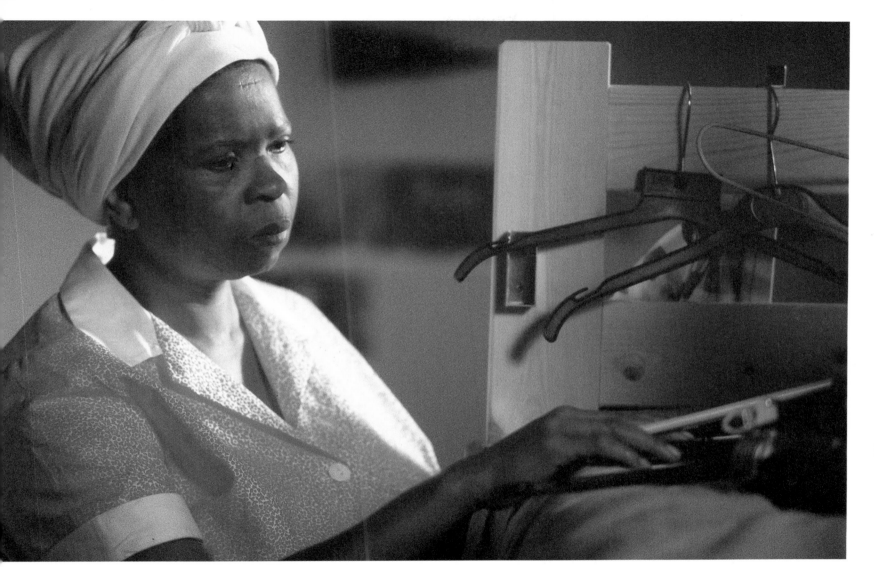

Empty cupboards puzzle Evalina.

While Wendy and the children make their
way to her parents' home . . .

Bruce drives towards the Lesotho capital at breakneck speed.

Donald confronts an astonished Acting British High
Commissioner in Maseru and asks to use the phone.

Wendy arrives just as her mother takes the call.

A triumphant Donald urges the family to make for the Telle River frontier as fast as possible.

At the South African border post their cover still
holds good.

Wendy and the five children walk towards Lesotho –
and exile – watched by her parents.

Donald, Wendy and the children are reunited at
Maseru airport.

Before boarding the small plane which is to fly them out of Lesotho, the Woods pose for a family photograph.

The Acting High Commissioner, his wife and the head of the charter company wave as the plane takes off. Bruce gives the Black Power salute.

In the air, under threat of being forced down by
South African patrol jets, Donald remembers Steve
and a conversation they had on 14 June 1976 . . .

Even Steve had no idea of the outcome when thousands of unarmed but well-organised and happy children took to the streets of Soweto that day. Many imbued with pride and self-reliance through the Black Consciousness Movement, they were protesting against the use of the Afrikaans language in their schools, peacefully demonstrating against a system of education blatantly designed to fit them for only the most menial jobs.

Then came confrontation with the authorities, warnings to disperse, tear gas. But, for the first time ever, the children of Soweto stood their ground. And the police opened fire. First to fall in the hail of bullets was Hector Petersen, aged just thirteen. In the violence which ensued, over four thousand Soweto children were wounded and more than five hundred killed by the police.

For a whole generation living in South Africa's townships nothing would ever be the same again. And when, in 1978, through the publication of Donald Wood's book, Steve Biko's story reached the outside world it became a rallying point in the struggle of decent people everywhere – black and white alike – to end the obscenity of apartheid.

CAST

Donald Woods: Kevin Kline
Wendy Woods: Penelope Wilton
Steve Biko: Denzel Washington
Bruce: John Hargreaves
Acting High Commissioner: Alec McCowen
Ken: Kevin McNally
Father Kani: Zakes Mokae
State Prosecutor: Ian Richardson
Dr Ramphele: Josette Simon
Kruger: John Thaw
Captain de Wet: Timothy West
Lemick: Miles Anderson
Tami: Tommy Buson
Peter Jones: Jim Findley
Don Card: Julian Glover
Jane Woods: Kate Hardie
Speaker: Alton Kumalo
Lesotho government official: Louis Mahoney
Jason: Mawa Makondo
Moses: Joseph Marcell
Mapetla: John Matshikiza
Evalina: Sophie Mgcina
Wendy's stepfather: John Paul
Tenjy: Wabei Siyolwe
Wendy's mother: Gwen Watford
Ntsiki Biko: Juanita Waterman
Dillon Woods: Graeme Taylor
Duncan Woods: Adam Stuart Walker
Gavin Woods: Hamish Stuart Walker
Mary Woods: Spring Stuart Walker

Nurses at clinic: Evelyn Sithole, Xoliswa Sithole
Young boy: James Coine
Alec: Albert Ndinda
Sub-Editor: Andrew Whaley
Woods's receptionist: Shelley Borkum
Shebeen queen: Patricia Gumede
Shebeen queen's niece: Angela Gavaza
Aunt: Nocebo Mlambo
Nephew: Walter Matemavi

Father: Clement Muchachi
Mother: Ruth Chinamando
Brother-in-law: Basil Chidyamathamba
Niece: Marcy Mushore
Informer: Lawrence Simbrashe
Policemen: Carl Chase, Morgan Sheppard
Dilima: Tichatonga Mazhindu
Lemick's assistant: Neil McPherson
Soga: Hepburn Graham
First rugby player: Claude Maredza
Second rugby player: Carlton Chance
First security guard: Glen Murphy
Second security guard: Russell Keith Grant
Samora Biko: Munyaradzi Kanaventi
Nkosinathi Biko: George Lovell
Policeman Nel: Andrew McCulloch
Nel's partner: Graham Fletcher Cook
Young secretary: Karen Drury
First roadblock policeman: Niven Boyd
Second roadblock policeman: Tony Vogel
Third roadblock policeman: Christopher Hurst
Police doctor: Gerald Sim
Senior police officer: Peter Cartwright
Police sergeant: Gary Whelan
Nationalist Party delegate: Dudley Dickin
Mortician: David Trevena
Mortician's assistant: Badi Uzzaman
Speaker at funeral: Robert Phillips
Biko's brother: Fishoo Tembo
'Helen Suzman': Peggy Marsh
Girl at funeral: Gwyneth Strong
Major Boshoff: Philip Bretherton
Beukes: Paul Herzberg
Security policemen: Robert MacNamara,
   Hans Sittig
Black security policeman: Kimpton Mativenga
Afrikaner farmer: David Henry
Judge Boshoff: Michael Turner
Magistrate Prins: Kalie Hanekom
Sergeant Louw: Paul Jerricho
First prisoner: Star Ncube

Second prisoner: David Guwaza
First passport control officer: Hilary Minister
Second passport control officer: James Aubrey
White frontier policeman: Peter Cary
Black frontier policeman: Dominic Kanaventi
Lesotho passport officer: Sam Mathambo
Lesotho businessman: Walter Muparutsa
Receptionist: Judy Cornwall
Third passport control officer: Michael
   Graham Cox
Fourth passport control officer: John Hartley
Young Lesotho official: Simon Shumba
McElrea: Garrick Hagon
Richie: Nick Tate
Acting High Commissioner's wife: Marilyn Poole
Police captain at Soweto: William Marlowe

PRODUCERS, DIRECTOR AND WRITER

Producer & Director: Richard Attenborough
Screenplay: John Briley
Executive producer in charge of production: Terence Clegg
Co-producers: Norman Spencer, John Briley

ADVISERS

Principal consultants: Donald Woods & Wendy Woods
Additional consultants: Hamilton Zolile Keke & Majakathata Mokoena
Special adviser to the director: Dalindlela Tambo

ART DEPARTMENT

Production designer: Stuart Craig
Supervising art directors: Norman Dorme, George Richardson
Art director: John King
Assistant art director: Gavin Bocquet
Set decorator: Michael Seirton
Buyers: Ian Giladjian, Lloyd Searle
Draughtsman: Mike Phillips
Sketch artist: Tony Wright

Construction managers: Bill Welch, Reg Richards
Assistant construction managers: Bert Long, Ian Mulder
Foreman: Terence Benson
Construction buyer: Jonathan Croesier

Prop master: Terry Wells
Chargehand standby prop: Michael Bacon
Standby props: Terry Wells Jnr.
Dressing props: Brian Humphrey, John Palmer
Storeman: Derek Knowler
Drapes: Roz Knight

Titles and optical effects: Geoff Axtell Associates

ON THE SET

First assistant director: David Tomblin
Script supervisor: Nikki Clapp

Co-first assistant director: Steve Chigorimbo
Assistant directors: Roy Button, Patrick Kinney, Steve Fillis
Third assistant directors: Sue Sheldon, Clive Stafford, David Bennett
Stunt co-ordinator: Peter Brace
Special effects supervisor: David Harris
Senior special effects technician: Martin Gant
Special effects technicians: Paul Knowles, Alan Poole, Gift Nyaniandi
Unit doctor: Dr. Keith Stack
Floor runner: Matthew Scudamore
Unit drivers: Vic Floyd, Lazarus Chingore

CAMERA

Director of photography: Ronnie Taylor, BSC
Camera operator: Eddie Collins
Focus: Jason Lehel
Clapper loader: Steve Burgess
Camera trainee: Richard Tindall
Chief grip: Jimmy Waters
Grips: David Chiganze, Peter Malunga
Gaffer: Alan Martin
Best boy: Dave Moore
Electricians: Dave McWhinnie, Tony Buckthorpe, Ricky Miller, Cephas Mathimba, Mathew Kausasa

SOUND

Sound recordist: Simon Kaye
Sound boom operator: Tommy Staples
Sound maintenance: Taffy Haines

MAKE-UP AND HAIRDRESSING

Make-up supervisor: Wally Schneiderman
Make-up artist: Beryl Lerman
Make-up assistant: Susan Haines

Hairdressers: Paula Gillespie, Vera Mitchell
Mr Kline's hair colour consultant: Daniel Galvin

WARDROBE

Costume designer: John Mollo
Wardrobe master: Kenny Crouch
Wardrobe mistress: Lisa Johnson
Wardrobe assistants: Andreas Fernandez Sotilos, Elaine Dawson,
  Virginia Mkiza

EDITING AND DUBBING

Film editor: Lesley Walker
Sound editor: Jonathan Bates
Dubbing mixer: Gerry Humphreys
First assistant editor: Jeremy Hume
Dialogue editors: Brian Mann, Mike Crouch
Footsteps editor: Chris Kelly
Second assistant editor: Kevin Lane
Assistant sound editors: Len Tremble, Steve Maguire
Editorial trainee: Andrew Melhuish
Assistant dubbing mixers: Dean Humphreys, Jonathan Frankel

MUSIC

Music: George Fenton & Jonas Gwangwa
Music score arranged and conducted by: George Fenton
Synthesisers: Ken Freeman
Vocal soloists: Thuli Dumakude, Nicola Emmanuel, Jonas Gwangwa
Additional orchestrations: Peter Whitehouse
Orchestral contractor: Isobel Griffiths
Recordist for Twickenham Music Studios: Keith Grant

CASTING

Casting director: Susie Figgis
Zimbabwe casting: Andrew Whaley
Crowd casting: Liz James

PUBLICITY

Director of marketing: Diana Hawkins
Stills photographers: Frank Connor, Simon Mein

Publicity specialist: Gillian Dobias
Publicity secretaries: Alison Webb, Zuzanne Whitehead

PRODUCTION OFFICE

Financial controller: John Trehy
Production managers: Allan James, Gerry Levy
Location manager: Rory Kilalea
Assistant location manager: Nandi Bowe
Transport manager: Arthur Dunne
Transport captain: Paul Fisher

Production co-ordinator: Judy Thornton
Assistant to Richard Attenborough: Clare Howard
Production assistant: Leila Kirkpatrick
Production secretaries: Marj Joscelyne, Marianne Jacobs
Film school attachment: Christopher J. O'Hare
Production runner: Mick Snell

Deputy accountant: Christine Samways
Studio accountant: Betty Williams
Location accountant: Michael Widd
Cashier: Eliah Fero
Production solicitors: Bartletts de Reya
Production accountants: Baker Rooke

SECOND UNIT

Director/Camerman: Peter Macdonald
Operator: John Campbell
Focus: David Rattenbury
Clapper/Loader: Adam Cooper
Continuity: Anne Wotton
Grip: Luke Quigley
Assistant directors: Steve Harding, Edwin Angless, Nikolas Korda
Prop: Ron Higgins
Gaffer: Steve Kitchen
Accounts: Craig Barwick
Special Photographer: Jody Boulting
Transport co-ordinator: Moncton Mutsvairo

Filmed in Panavision ®

Processed by Rank Film Laboratories Ltd. ®

Filmed principally in the
Republic of Zimbabwe,
and completed in Kenya, the United Kingdom
and at Lee International Film Studios Ltd, Shepperton, England
with post-production at Twickenham Studios, Middlesex, England.

British Library Cataloguing in Publication Data. Attenborough, Richard Cry freedom. 1. Cry freedom (Motion-picture) I. Title
791.43'72   PN1997.C86/ISBN 0-370-31161-2 ISBN 0-370-31158-2 Pbk

Printed and bound in Great Britain for The Bodley Head Ltd, 32 Bedford Square, London WC1B 3EL by W.S. Cowell
Ltd, Ipswich, Suffolk. Set in Ehrhardt by Hope Services Ltd, Oxford

First published 1987